CONNECTING TO THE GOD OF BREAKTHROUGHS

DR. D. K. OLUKOYA

(2) Dr. D. K. OLUKOYA

CONNECTING TO THE GOD OF BREAKTHROUGHS
© 2009 DR. D. K. OLUKOYA
ISBN 978-978-49178-1-0
October 2009

Published by:
The Battle Cry Christian Ministries
322, Herbert Macaulay Way, Yaba P. O. Box 12272, Ikeja, Lagos.
website: www.battlecrychristianministries.org
email: info@battlecrychristianministries.org
Phone: 234(0)8033044239, 234(0)8033060073.

All Scripture quotation is from the King James Version of the Bible

All rights reserved.
We prohibit reproduction in whole or part without written permission.

TABLE OF CONTENTS

The Mystery Of Turn-Around Breakthroughs 4

Connecting To The God Of Breakthroughs . 14

Cases Of Turn-Around Breakthroughs . . 21

A Complete Turn-Around 29

Keys To Turn-Around Breakthroughs . . . 45

(4) Dr. D. K. OLUKOYA

CHAPTER ONE

THE MYSTERY OF TURN-AROUND BREAKTHROUGHS

CONNECTING TO THE GOD OF BREAKTHROUGHS (5)

Hast thou not known? hast thou not heard, that the everlasting God, the LORD, the Creator of the ends of the earth, fainteth not, neither is weary? there is no searching of his understanding. He giveth power to the faint; and to them that have no might he increaseth strength. Even the youths shall faint and be weary, and the young men shall utterly fall: But they that wait upon the LORD shall renew their strength; they shall mount up with wings as eagles; they shall run, and not be weary; and they shall walk, and not faint. (Isa 40:28-31)

There is a season in life when all you need is a supernatural turn-around. There are situations in life when the best of our efforts end up in futility. At such times we need a special connection to the God of turn-around. God specializes in doing the impossible in order to make the incredible become achievable.

We come to our wits end when we have made all efforts. Millions all over the world have spent fortunes to procure solutions to life's problems. But the more efforts are made the more intractable human conditions become. Our best can never be good enough without divine assistance. What we need is divine connection which will turn around stubborn or impossible situations.

DIVINE CONNECTION

The good news is that God is a God of miraculous turn-around. When situations become so awful that men and women give up in despair, that is not the end of the story. Connecting to the God of turn-around will change your story to glory, your tears to rejoicing and your struggles to moments of celebration.

And the Gentiles shall see thy righteousness, and all kings thy glory: and thou shalt be called by a new name, which the mouth of the LORD shall name. Thou shalt also be a crown of glory in the hand of the LORD, and a royal diadem in the hand of thy God. Thou shalt no more be termed Forsaken; neither shall thy land any more be termed Desolate: but thou shalt be called Hephzibah, and thy land Beulah: for the LORD

delighteth in thee, and thy land shall be married. (Isa 62:2-4)

No matter what your condition looks like at the moment, God is ready to turn it around. We serve the God who specializes in turning hopeless situations around.

A NEW BEGINNING

I am yet to see a condition that can be termed hopeless, which God cannot turn around. One of the most interesting things in life is to experience a turn-around. When men and women conclude that all hope is lost, God begins afresh.

THE MYSTERY OF TURN-AROUND

A turn-around is a situation of completely positive change, the reversal of a situation that was previously undesirable. The following areas of turn-around are achievable.

(8) Dr. D. K. OLUKOYA

1. Spiritual turn-around.

You can experience a turn-around in your spiritual life after a long bout of spiritual dryness, spiritual famine, lethargy and a state of spiritual deadness. A soul that has gone away from the Lord can suddenly experience revival. Someone who had maintained a close walk with the Lord and then went into the wilderness can experience a turn-around through a life-changing spiritual rejuvenation. If there is any area where we need a turn-around it is our spiritual life.

The index of your spirituality is a sound commentary on the totality of your well-being. Our God takes delight in turning the spiritual lives of his sons and daughter around. No matter how far you are from God, He can give you a turn-around that will literally transform your life.

Repent ye therefore, and be converted, that your sins may be blotted out, when the times of refreshing shall come from the presence of the Lord; (Act 3:19)

2. Marital turn-around.

There are people who go through crisis, tragedy and unpleasant situations in their marital lives. Many couples are almost heading for the courts to file divorce suits. Many who are not contemplating divorced are living in the same house as cats and rats.

A lot of bachelors and spinsters have given up on themselves, thinking that marriage would ever remain an illusion. Many have had series of broken engagements, failed attempts at getting married. A lot of couples are battling with childlessness. Of course, there are situations where parents are struggling with delinquent children.

Many people cry day and night for turn-around in the family. The moment the God of turn-around touches your marital life, everything changes.

Look unto me, and be ye saved, all the ends of the earth: for I am God, and there is none else. I have sworn by myself, the word is gone out of my mouth in righteousness, and shall not return, That unto me every knee shall bow, every tongue

shall swear. Surely, shall one say, in the LORD have I righteousness and strength: even to him shall men come; and all that are incensed against him shall be ashamed. In the LORD shall all the seed of Israel be justified, and shall glory. (Isa 45:22-25)

The moment the God of turn-around arises, those who never thought they could get married will become happily married, childless couples will give birth to glorious children and all kinds of stubborn problems will disappear. There will be testimonies galore in the family. Barren women will become joyful mothers, frustrated husbands will be blessed with the means of raising blessed families, while there will be heaven in several homes.

3. Financial turn-around.

We live in an era when financial insufficiency is the dominant problem. The condition in several quarters leaves much to be desired. Most people are going through hard times, but when a financial turn-around occurs, those who were once struggling to make ends meet will be bombarded with financial surplus. When God links you with the hidden treasures, money will keep flooding your house and your business ventures.

God will continue to load you with financial blessings on daily basis. Whatever you touch will turn to gold. Your expectations will be fulfilled. You will make minimal efforts and reap maximum profits. Termites that eat up people's finances will be swept away from your domain. God Himself will open unto you his good treasure.

When you knock at one door, seven will be opened unto you. God will bless your baskets, enrich your accounts and prosper the work of your hands. You will get to a point in your finances when you will require additional help to calculate your gains.

The God of turn-around has declared, "Silver and gold is mine." When God decides to lavish his wealth upon your life, you will begin to wonder whether you are the only one who knows how to make money.

And I will give thee the treasures of darkness, and hidden riches of secret places, that thou

mayest know that I, the LORD, which call thee by thy name, am the God of Israel. (Isa 45:3)

4. Career turn-around.

A lot of people are unable to make it in their chosen fields. Many people have pursued academics and have not been able to succeed. Some have not been able to succeed in the professions which they have been trained. But the God of fulfilment is the only one who can give you a complete turn-around in your career or profession. When God gives you a career turn-around, you will shine like a star.

Your professional competence will become a wonder to your contemporaries. God will give you the anointing of excellence and there will be a sudden turn-around in your career. What others struggle to achieve in ten years will become achievable for you within one year.

God himself will be at work in your career. His help will be available and you will succeed without sweating unnecessarily.

CONNECTING TO THE GOD OF BREAKTHROUGHS (13)
LIFE-CHANGING TURN-AROUND

This is the type of turn-around that takes place once and changes the rest of your history. When you get connected to the God of turn-around, a single experience will become your reference point. From that moment people will begin to wonder what you did or what happened to you to make you experience such amazing changes. God does not need to spend eternity in order to give you a life-changing turn-around. One event is just enough. One miracle is enough to change your history.

One breakthrough is enough to feed you and your generation. One blessing is enough to make your entire lineage blessed forever. All you need is to have a connection with the God who gives the type of turn-around that leaves people wondering.

CHAPTER TWO

CONNECTING TO THE GOD OF BREAKTHROUGHS

CONNECTING TO THE GOD OF BREAKTHROUGHS (15)

The LORD killeth, and maketh alive: he bringeth down to the grave, and bringeth up. The LORD maketh poor, and maketh rich: he bringeth low, and lifteth up. He raiseth up the poor out of the dust, and lifteth up the beggar from the dunghill, to set them among princes, and to make them inherit the throne of glory: for the pillars of the earth are the LORD'S, and he hath set the world upon them. (1Sa 2:6-8)

God raises from one extreme to the other. He lifts up the poor and makes him a prince and lifts up the beggar from the dunghill to the throne.

For promotion cometh neither from the east, nor from the west, nor from the south. But God is the judge: he putteth down one, and setteth up another. (Psa 75:6-7)

I decree that anything that must be put down for you to rise, the Lord shall put them down, in the name of Jesus.

Read the following:

1. The change that will move your life forward is

not a plastic change but a change from the inside.

2. You can turn your life around. God has given you the capacity to do so and the choice now belongs to you.

3. When you get to the top you will become a topic.

4. Any man or woman who is comfortable in Egypt will never get to the promised land. It is time you become uncomfortable with the level you are now.

5. You can move from negativity to positivity.

6. The Bible is full of turn-around.

7. The Almighty God is a God of turn-around.

The Bible is full of turn-around stories. Abraham's story was that of a turn-around. He was an unknown idol worshipper in Ur of the Caldeas. This unknown idol worshipper now underwent a turn-around and became a worshipper of the true God. This complete turn-around that took place in his life made people to marvel.

CONNECTING TO THE GOD OF BREAKTHROUGHS (17)

A particular woman had to hawk four times a day so as to be able to feed her family. All of a sudden, she experienced a turn-around and at present she has nothing less than seven cars. There was a day she was supposed to deliver a paper and people were arguing that she was not the same old person who used to hawk four times each day in their street. I pray that your promotion shall confuse your enemies, in the name of Jesus Your breakthrough shall become a debate.

CLASSIC EXAMPLES

Moses' story was that of a turn-around from a murderer to a deliverer. Moses was commissioned at the age of 80 to work for God. No matter what your age is, God can still use you.

Ruth, in the Bible, had an unenviable root but accompanied her mother-in-law, Naomi, to Israel. She moved from being a lonely widow to becoming a happily married lady. God is the God of turn-around.

Rahab, in the Bible, was in the abominable

profession of prostitution. But she eventually connected with the God of turn-around. Rahab eventually became the progenitor of the Lord Jesus Christ. This means that you can start the journey of your life from the wrong side of the road but God can re-position you for a complete change.

One day, while I was in the plane, as I was going to the toilet after eating, I saw the hostess who had served us food, sitting at the back and praying from the Prayer Rain. As soon as I saw her I started smiling. Soon somebody told her that I was the author of the book she was praying from. She rushed to me and asked me if I was Dr. Olukoya. I told her yes.

She asked if I needed anything and I told her no. This sister, whom I had not known, told me that she was formerly a cripple, that it was at one of our Power Must Change Hands meetings that the Lord touched her. Today, she is an hostess. This is indeed an example of a turn-around breakthrough. I pray that the Lord shall arise for your sake, in the name of Jesus.

CONNECTING TO THE GOD OF BREAKTHROUGHS (19)

TO GOD ALL THINGS ARE POSSIBLE

The Bible does not even bother to tell us who the mother of David was. And his father did not consider him as one of his important sons and would not have voted for him if he had stood for an election. However, this unknown shepherd boy became a deliverer king. This was a turn-around. If the enemy has been telling you that your situation will remain the same forever, that enemy is a lair.

Esther was a slave girl but later became a queen, the wife of a man who could be regarded as the king of the whole world. This was a turn-around breakthrough.

Zacheus in the New Testament was a crook but later became a generous giver. You can be the worst crook but if you surrender to Jesus, He can still turn your life around.

Paul was a persecutor of Christians, but this same person eventually became a church planter and wrote 13 epistles.

You can therefore see that the Bible is rife with

records of God's turn-around activities.

That God of Abraham, Moses, Esther, David, etc. is still the same God today. Unfortunately our Christianity has moved far away from what God recommended.

Many people still don't understand that when you surrender to Jesus you have complete transformation. The ministry of Jesus is a turn-around ministry. His first miracle was to turn water to wine.

The Spirit of the Lord is upon me, because he hath anointed me to preach the gospel to the poor; he hath sent me to heal the brokenhearted, to preach deliverance to the captives, and recovering of sight to the blind, to set at liberty them that are bruised,

You can call the above passage the manifesto of the gospel. It is probably the most powerful turn-around verse in the Scripture. You might have been born in a manger but you don't have to sit and suffer in silence.

CHAPTER THREE
CASES OF TURN-AROUND BREAKTHROUGHS

ABRAHAM'S TURN-AROUND

Abraham had a life changing turn-around. He was an ordinary man by all standards. He had an experience with God which made him the father of many nations. He had a single encounter with God and God told him that his children would be like the stars of the firmament and the sand of the sea.

And the angel of the LORD called unto him out of heaven, and said, Abraham, Abraham: and he said, Here am I. And he said, Lay not thine hand upon the lad, neither do thou any thing unto him: for now I know that thou fearest God, seeing thou hast not withheld thy son, thine only son from me. And Abraham lifted up his eyes, and looked, and behold behind him a ram caught in a thicket by his horns: and Abraham went and took the ram, and offered him up for a burnt offering in the stead of his son. And Abraham called the name of that place Jehovahjireh: as it is said to this day, In the mount of the LORD it shall be seen. And the angel of the LORD called unto Abraham out of heaven the second time, And said, By myself have

I sworn, saith the LORD, for because thou hast done this thing, and hast not withheld thy son, thine only son: That in blessing I will bless thee, and in multiplying I will multiply thy seed as the stars of the heaven, and as the sand which is upon the sea shore; and thy seed shall possess the gate of his enemies; And in thy seed shall all the nations of the earth be blessed; because thou hast obeyed my voice. (Gen 22:11-18)

JACOB'S EXPERIENCE

Jacob had a life-changing turn-around. He had a vision where he saw angels ascending and descending. From that moment his name changed to Israel.

And God said unto Jacob, Arise, go up to Bethel, and dwell there: and make there an altar unto God, that appeared unto thee when thou fleddest from the face of Esau thy brother. Then Jacob said unto his household, and to all that were with him, Put away the strange gods that are among you, and be clean, and change your garments: And let us arise, and go up to Bethel; and I will make there an altar unto God, who answered me in the day of my distress, and was with me in the way which I went. And they gave unto Jacob all the strange gods which were in their hand, and all their earrings which were in their ears; and Jacob hid them under the oak which was by Shechem. And they journeyed: and the terror of God was upon the cities that were round about them, and they did not pursue after the sons of Jacob. So Jacob came to Luz, which is in the land of Canaan, that is, Bethel, he and all the people that were with him. And he built there an altar, and called the place Elbethel: because there God appeared unto him, when he fled from the face of his brother. But Deborah Rebekah's nurse died, and she was buried beneath Bethel under an oak: and the name of it was called Allonbachuth. And God appeared unto Jacob again, when he came out of Padanaram, and blessed him. And God said unto him, Thy name is Jacob: thy name shall not be called any more Jacob, but

Israel shall be thy name: and he called his name Israel. And God said unto him, I am God Almighty: be fruitful and multiply; a nation and a company of nations shall be of thee, and kings shall come out of thy loins; And the land which I gave Abraham and Isaac, to thee I will give it, and to thy seed after thee will I give the land. And God went up from him in the place where he talked with him. And Jacob set up a pillar in the place where he talked with him, even a pillar of stone: and he poured a drink offering thereon, and he poured oil thereon. And Jacob called the name of the place where God spake with him, Bethel. (Gen 35:1-15)

AN UNUSUAL CATCH

Peter and other disciples also had a life-changing turn-around. In one fishing expedition Peter and his colleagues had an unusual catch which made them to seek the assistance of their friends to bring their large haul ashore. The Bible tells us that the catch was so heavy that their boat sank.

And it came to pass, that, as the people pressed upon him to hear the word of God, he stood by the lake of Gennesaret. And saw two ships standing by the lake: but the fishermen were gone out of them, and were washing their nets. And he entered into one of the ships, which was Simon's, and prayed him that he would thrust out a little from the land. And he sat down, and taught the people out of the ship. Now when he had left speaking, he said unto Simon, Launch out into the deep, and let down your nets for a draught. And Simon answering said unto him, Master, we have toiled all the night, and have taken nothing: nevertheless at thy word I will let down the net. And when they had this done, they inclosed a great multitude of fishes: and their net brake. And they beckoned unto their partners, which were in the other ship, that they should come and help them. And they came, and filled both the ships, so that they began to sink. (Luk 5:1-7)

What you need from God are not miracles that will come in trickles. You need one uncommon miracle and your story will never remain the same. You need to pray that God should visit you once in such a manner as to make you a reference point. When God does something unusual in your life, even if you lived in an isolated village, the whole world will troop out to look for you.

JUST ONE CONNECTION

You should pray for divine turn-around. When this happens, your struggles will be over, your tears will vanish, your sighing will stop, your sorrow will melt away and all forms of discouragement will become a thing of the past. Just one connection to the God of turn-around will change your situation and rewrite your history.

APOSTOLIC MIRACLES

When God makes you a recipient of his turn-around you will begin to experience miracles, signs and wonders. Let me say this at this point: one of the high points of the revelation given to us at the inception of MFM is that we would encounter God on the mountain, the fire of God will be palpable, and the result will be apostolic miracles. This explains why we have been known for astonishing miracles and wonders.

The God whom we encounter on the mountain specializes in turning around destinies. I have come across people at home and abroad who have achieved greatness in spite of being written off before they came in contact with the God of Mountain of Fire and Miracle Ministries. My head has often exploded with joy when I heard testimonies of men and women who later began to shine after their virtues had been buried by witchcraft and household wickedness.

The God of Mountain of Fire and Miracles Ministries is the God who turns around destinies. You cannot spend three months on the mountain without having an encounter with the God of turn-around.

No matter the level of breakthroughs you have experienced, God has just started with you. You have not seen anything yet. The best is yet to come.

CHAPTER FOUR

A COMPLETE TURN-AROUND

The story of Moses is a classic example of what it takes to experience a turn-around miracle. Moses was someone who could have been described as an underdog. He rose from the status of an outcast and became a deliverer. He spent 40 years in the desert and was actually forgotten during that 40 long years.

There were no events and no celebrations that brought him to limelight. When he was spending those years as a fugitive, he never realized that he would one day walk gallantly to the palace of Pharaoh and confront the monarch. Nobody ever thought that he would one day speak in the palace of Pharaoh. God commissioned him to work for Him at an age when it is normally impossible to amount to anything.

He was a stammer and his speech impairment apparently disqualified him, but we serve a God who qualifies the unqualified. As it were God brought Moses from the backseat to the front seat. An outcast became the leader of more than three million Jews.

Moses became a terror to the dictator called

Pharaoh. His words became law. The condemned became the lawgiver. The stammerer became a man whose words brought chill down the spine of despotic Pharaoh. Our God is wonderful.

Which doeth great things past finding out; yea, and wonders without number. (Job 9:10)

O the depth of the riches both of the wisdom and knowledge of God! how unsearchable are his judgments, and his ways past finding out! (Rom 11:33)

A DIVINE SPECIMEN

Moses became an example of how far God can go in transforming destinies. No matter your condition today, God can take you from the lowest point to the highest point. Moses overcame the impediments which are common to men. He had a criminal record; he had to flee after an incident of murder.

But when God's hands touched his destiny, he did not have to struggle with his handicapped areas. This tells us that God can single out as monuments of excellence even those who are physically challenged or those who have had dark areas in their history. No matter what you have gone through, no matter how many negative leaders you passed through, when God touches your destiny, the same people who once castigated you will be forced to celebrate your breakthrough.

ESTHER'S TURN-AROUND

The story of Esther reminds us of the fact that those who were born in or raised from lowly backgrounds can be exalted to high status in life. Nobody can ever imagine that a slave girl could rise to the position of the queen of one of the greatest empires in Bible history. Esther was grappling with the shackles of slavery and could move nowhere near her exalted predecessor, queen Vashti. She might have only dreamt of the throne of the queen.

She could not go near the precincts of the opulent palace. But in a twist of circumstances, queen Vashti was removed and God brought a slave girl to inherit what the proud queen lost. Esther could only depend on God. She declared, "If I perish, I perish." God demoted queen Vashti and installed the slave girl Esther. This is a turn-around miracle.

Now it came to pass on the third day, that Esther put on her royal apparel, and stood in the inner court of the king's house, over against the king's house: and the king sat upon his royal throne in the royal house, over against the gate of the house. And it was so, when the king saw Esther the queen standing in the court, that she obtained favour in his sight: and the king held out to Esther the golden sceptre that was in his hand. So Esther drew near, and touched the top of the sceptre. Then said the king unto her, What wilt thou, queen Esther? and what is thy request? it shall be even given thee to the half of the kingdom. (Est 5:1-3)

PAUL'S TRANSFORMATION

The story of Paul the apostle bears eloquent

testimony to the fact that there is no point you can get to in life where the power and the grace of God cannot turn your situation around. Paul is one Bible character miraculously transformed by God. A persecutor became a saint. Someone who hated Christianity became one of the most vocal advocates of Christianity.

Though I might also have confidence in the flesh. If any other man thinketh that he hath whereof he might trust in the flesh, I more: Circumcised the eighth day, of the stock of Israel, of the tribe of Benjamin, an Hebrew of the Hebrews; as touching the law, a Pharisee; Concerning zeal, persecuting the church; touching the righteousness which is in the law, blameless. But what things were gain to me, those I counted loss for Christ. Yea doubtless, and I count all things but loss for the excellency of the knowledge of Christ Jesus my Lord: for whom I have suffered the loss of all things, and do count them but dung, that I may win Christ, And be found in him, not having mine own righteousness, which is of the law, but that which is through the faith of Christ, the righteousness which is of God by faith: That I may know him, and the power of his resurrection, and the fellowship of his sufferings, being made conformable unto his death; If by any means I might attain unto the resurrection of the dead. Not as though I had already attained, either were already perfect: but I follow after, if that I may apprehend that for which also I am apprehended of Christ Jesus. (Php 3:4-12)

Paul the apostle was busy spitting fire and breathing cruelty against Jesus' disciples. He hated the name of Christ and vowed to deal with the believers of his day.

One day, God turned his life around and his entire situation became reversed. He became a defender of the Name he once castigated. He became a slave of the gospel he once detested. He became an advocate of the Good News he once tore to shreds.

All his intelligence and training were turned to the propagation of the gospel. A man who once thought that Christians were foolish vowed to spend and be spent for the cause of the gospel. The turn-around he experienced was so encompassing that his life has become a great challenge to all believers in all ages. The God of turn-around completely transformed his life and destiny. Paul became an instrument for presenting to the whole world the glorious hope that is in the gospel.

A GREAT CHANGE

Through Paul we discover that when you have an encounter with the God of turn-around, your life would change. Your life will be so changed that everyone will begin to marvel. How could a man who was a first class persecutor become a prominent apostle? How could a man who obtained letters of authority to deal with believers become a writer of 13 epistles to encourage believers?

How could a man whose initial mission was to destroy churches become a tireless church planter? How could a man who once thought that Christianity was folly become the man who decided to count every other thing in life as dung and dross? How could a man who went out looking for believers to kill become an apostle who was ready to lay down his life for the sake of the gospel? How could a man at whose feet those who lynched believers cast their garments become a man who risked his life while declaring the same gospel? This is a mystery of divine turn-around.

IT IS NOT HOPELESS

A turn-around miracle is what you need to calm your anxious nerves. When God gives you a turn-around, your fears are gone, impossibilities disappear and hopelessness vanishes. God takes delight in manifesting His power when human cases appear hopeless. It takes a great problem to experience a great miracle. The tougher your trials appear the more pronounced the miracle power of God would be.

Unless there is a significant change, you cannot talk of a turn-around. The difference between your previous condition and the circumstances in which you find yourself, should be pronounced enough to project the awesome power of God. You cannot appreciate the greatness of the power of God if there is no storm.

A GREAT STORM

During the ministry of the Lord Jesus Christ, there was an instance of a great storm. The storm was so violent that the disciples felt that their lives were in jeopardy. But Jesus, the Master of oceans and seas, spoke with authority and there was a total calm.

The devil thought he could destabilize the disciples. He had miscalculated, he never thought that their problem could become their miracle. The magnitude of the storm became an opportunity of appreciating the power of God that was able to save to the uttermost. The devil often makes mistakes when he brings up an ugly situation. He paves a way for God to manifest His power and His glory.

The storm became a miracle. Through it the disciples were made to appreciate the presence of the King of kings and the Lord of lords who was with them. The devil still makes the same mistakes today, he comes with a situation that appears very helpless, only to give us opportunity to demonstrate the fact that there is no situation which our God cannot turn around.

A DIVINE DRAMA

A turn-around is a divine drama. It shows God in action. There will be no testimonies without instances of turn-around. You need a turn-around to move ahead in life. You need to take cognizance of the fact that if there are no problems there would be no turn-around.

It is important to take note of the fact that when you are confronted by a challenge you have a fresh opportunity to prove to the whole world that the God of the whole world is still on the throne. You will at that point join the company of celebrated Bible characters whose names have been displayed in the hall of faith.

(40) Dr. D. K. OLUKOYA

THE HALL OF FAITH

The 11th chapter of the book of Hebrew contains records of men and women who experienced turn-around breakthroughs. These characters rose out of obscurity, overcame ugly challenges and stood out to validate the claim of the Scripture.

By faith Abraham, when he was called to go out into a place which he should after receive for an inheritance, obeyed; and he went out, not knowing whither he went. By faith he sojourned in the land of promise, as in a strange country, dwelling in tabernacles with Isaac and Jacob, the heirs with him of the same promise: For he looked for a city which hath foundations, whose builder and maker is God. Through faith also Sara herself received strength to conceive seed, and was delivered of a child when she was past age, because she judged him faithful who had promised. Therefore sprang there even of one, and him as good as dead, so many as the stars of the sky in multitude, and as the sand which is by the sea shore innumerable. These all died in faith, not having received the promises, but having seen them afar off, and were persuaded of them, and embraced them, and confessed that they were strangers and pilgrims on the earth. For they that say such things declare plainly that they seek a country. And truly, if they had been mindful of that country from whence they came out, they might have had opportunity to have returned. But now they desire a better country, that is, an heavenly: wherefore God is not ashamed to be called their God: for he hath prepared for them a city. By faith Abraham, when he was tried, offered up Isaac: and he that had received the promises offered up his only begotten son, Of whom it was said, That in Isaac shall thy seed be called: Accounting that God was able to raise him up, even from the dead; from whence also he received him in a figure. By faith Isaac blessed Jacob and Esau concerning things to come. By faith Jacob, when he was a dying, blessed both the sons of Joseph; and worshipped, leaning upon the top of his staff. By faith Joseph, when he died, made mention of the departing of the children of Israel; and gave commandment concerning his bones. By faith Moses, when he was born, was hid three months of his parents, because they saw he was a proper child; and they were not afraid of the king's commandment. By faith Moses, when he was come to years, refused to be called the son of Pharaoh's daughter; Choosing rather to suffer affliction with the people of God, than to enjoy the pleasures of sin for a season; Esteeming the reproach of Christ greater riches than the treasures in Egypt: for he had respect unto the recompence of the reward. By faith he forsook Egypt, not fearing the wrath of the king: for he endured, as seeing him who is invisible. Through faith he kept the passover, and the sprinkling of blood, lest he that destroyed the firstborn should touch them. By faith they passed through the Red sea as by dry land: which the Egyptians assaying to do were drowned. By faith the walls of Jericho fell down, after they were compassed about seven days. By faith the harlot Rahab perished not with them that believed not, when she had received the spies with peace. And what shall I more say? for the time would fail me to tell of Gedeon, and of Barak, and of Samson, and of Jephthae; of David also, and Samuel, and of the prophets: Who through faith subdued kingdoms, wrought righteousness, obtained promises, stopped the mouths of lions, Quenched the violence of fire, escaped the edge of the sword, out of weakness were made strong, waxed valiant in fight, turned to flight the armies of the aliens. (Heb 11:8-34)

These Bible characters came up with outstanding achievements. There is a common denominator in their experiences; they had individual encounters with the God of turn-around breakthroughs. Majority of them was weak but they drew from the strength of the Almighty. God came into their situations and demonstrated the fullness of His power.

There was a wonderful interplay of strength and weakness, hope and despair, abundance and lack, fear and boldness as well as interplay of human extremity and divine opportunity. The divine exchange made those who would never have made it to become celebrated stars. God proved Himself in the lives of men and women whose names were penciled among the great of the 11th chapter of the book of Hebrews.

When you consider the story of each character, you will discover that it is representative of the condition of the average man in this generation. God has proved to us for the umpteenth time that His omnipotence will always bail us out in our human limitations.

CHAPTER FIVE

KEYS TO TURN-AROUND BREAKTHROUGHS

In this chapter we shall examine the seven keys needed to connect to the God of turn around breakthroughs. Life is not about struggles. When you come across the right key, the most sophisticated doors will be thrown wide open. Struggling without succeeding will lead to frustration, but when God puts the keys to turn around breakthrough, you will benefit from the anointing of ease.

The anointing of ease comes when God puts an end to your struggles. You will no longer need to profit from excessive sweating. A little effort will yield great results. God can give you a simple idea which will remove you from the class of those who struggle from dawn to dusk without anything to show for it. God will envelope you in His favour and make you to swim in the ocean of grace.

THE KEYS

With the seven keys in your hands, no situation in life will baffle you, no challenge in life will make you to tremble and no circumstance will make your heart to fear.

You will become as bold as a lion. You will so depend on the sufficiency of the Almighty that you will no longer need to spend donkey years struggling to earn a living. God Himself will throw His treasure house wide open to you. You will walk in and make use of that which pertains to life and godliness. All the blessings which you require will be placed at your disposal. God will overwhelm you with grace, bombard you with favour and lavish His divine benevolence upon your life. With these keys in your hands, you will no longer remain the same.

Let us go through the keys one after the other:

1. Make God your friend

The first step, which you must take to connect to the God of turn-around breakthroughs is to make God your friend. You cannot benefit from God if you are a stranger to Him. His blessings are meant for His children. You must be born again. You need to become a child of God in order to benefit from all that He has to offer. The born again experience makes you a recipient of all the benefits of the kingdom of God.

This initial experience places you at a vantage point. You must experience a change of location if you want to receive the key to divine turn-around. You need to come out from the kingdom of darkness and get into the kingdom of God through the new birth experience. Your salvation must be genuine if you want to make use of a key that is genuine.

Your new birth experience must be thorough and complete. There are fewer cases of turn around experiences in many churches today simply because the majority does not know what it takes to be soundly converted. It is unfortunate that many people who sing and dance in churches today are simply not born again. A lot of people are eager to receive miracles. But they neglect the greatest of all miracles, the miracle of salvation.

The truth is that you cannot receive enduring miracles from God if you have not received the miracle of salvation. I have stated this time and again that God is not under any obligation to bless those who are not His children. If you have no connection with the God of turn-around breakthrough through the act of sonship, you cannot experience real divine turn-around.

2. *Genuine repentance.*

Perhaps you are wondering how you can make God your friend. This can only be achieved through genuine repentance. If you continue to live a sinful life, you will remain an enemy of God. The Bible says that God is always angry with the sinners. If you want to experience the favour of God, you must start with true repentance. Every genuine turn-around starts with repentance.

Repent ye therefore, and be converted, that your sins may be blotted out, when the times of refreshing shall come from the presence of the Lord; Act 3:19.

Repentance means a change of heart. God cannot do anything with you until you fully repent. When He wants to change your situation He calls you into repentance. The moment you heed the call to repentance He begins afresh with you. Repentance goes beyond weeping over your sins. It entails total change of life. You must be prepared to make an about-turn and begin to say 'no' to the dictates of the flesh and 'yes' to the dictates of the Holy Spirit. Fake repentance will lead to fake breakthroughs.

When your repentance is weak, your spiritual life is weak. Lack of repentance will invite the enemy into your life. When you fail to repent, you are throwing an open invitation to the enemy to attack you. To repent you must drop all your sinful habits. Every habit that answers to the dictates of the flesh will make the door of your breakthrough to remain closed. Your habit will become your greatest helper or your greatest burden. Sinful habit will drag you down to the valley of failure and the removal of it will lead you to the mountain top. Repent today and you will be amazed at what God will do for you.

3. Disconnect from your old ways.

If you want to be connected to the God of turn-around breakthroughs, you must be ready to sever all old, useless ways. Old ways will make the keys of turn-around breakthroughs not to function. As long as you are still connected to your old ways and lifestyles, you will not experience divine connection to the God of turn-around breakthroughs.

Until you remove the old, you cannot embrace the new. If you keep celebrating achievements that are worthless, you will not experience new breakthroughs. You must learn how to disconnect from people who will pull you back to your old ways.

If you want to be connected to the Source of Power, you must disconnect from the source of powerlessness. You have the option of remaining the way you are or getting connected to God who specializes in making all things new. The choice is yours: between the source of pure water and remaining connected to broken cisterns that cannot hold any water.

If you do not say 'bye' to the old, the new will never come. If you do not surrender your shallowness, God's fullness cannot come. You must disconnect, if you want to be connected in a genuine manner.

4. You must carry out generational deliverance.

No one is an island: You are a product of your ancestors. You come from a particular lineage where there are lots of bondages. If it has been declared that your lineage will never experience turn-around breakthrough, you must remove yourself from such deadly, umbrella bondage.

You need to go through generational deliverance. You must eliminate your name from the list of those who are under a curse or curses in your generation. You must deliberately go through deliverance to get rid of generational bondage. There are some turn-around breakthroughs that can never be yours unless your go through generational deliverance. This deliverance will become a key that will open spiritual warehouses where your blessings are stored.

5. Take steps to renew your mind.

The renewal of the mind is an important key necessary for experiencing divine turn-around. Your mind will either open you up to a world of opportunity, or it will lock you up in a prison house.

CONNECTING TO THE GOD OF BREAKTHROUGHS

You can go only as far as your mind can allow you. A negative mindset will keep you in a backward position in life, while a positive mindset will lead you into the realm of limitless possibilities. You can only renew your mind when the word of God washes and refreshes your heart. The need for renewal of the mind is made plain in the Scriptures.

The Bible says: "Let the word of Christ dwell richly within me." We are challenged to renew our minds on a continual basis. Your inner man needs constant renewal.

The law of the LORD is perfect, converting the soul: the testimony of the LORD is sure, making wise the simple. The statutes of the LORD are right, rejoicing the heart: the commandment of the LORD is pure, enlightening the eyes. The fear of the LORD is clean, enduring for ever: the judgments of the LORD are true and righteous altogether. More to be desired are they than gold, yea, than much fine gold: sweeter also than honey and the honeycomb. Moreover by them is thy servant warned: and in keeping of them there is great reward. (Psa 19:7-11)

Only the word of God can work on your mind successfully and renew it to be prepared for what it takes to possess your possession. The task of renewing your mind must not be done haphazardly.

You must keep working on your mind until it has attained the status meant for those who want to experience divine turn-around. The renewal of the mind does not thrive on a hit or miss method. After you have renewed your mind, you must keep it in that renewed state.

The greatest battle, which the enemy fights, takes place in the battlefield of the mind. If he succeeds in making your mind a rubbish heap, you will not be able to possess your possession or experience the turn-around breakthrough you are praying for. Remember your life or destiny rises or falls on the basis of your mind. This explains why the Bible says: "Keep your heart with all diligence; for out of it are issues of life."

6. You must pray enquiry prayers.

There is a type of prayer which leads to revelation. When you pray such a prayer God opens your eyes and you see deep and wondrous things. Turn-around breakthrough is nearer to you more than you can imagine.

Call unto me, and I will answer thee, and shew thee great and mighty things, which thou knowest not. (Jer 33:3)

You only need to pray in order to see the angels waiting on you to lead you to your turn-around miracles. Do not go through life without a clear understanding of what you were meant to be and achieve. When you pray, God would show you the turn-around breakthroughs that heaven has earmarked for you. When your eyes are open, you are able to pray to hit the targets destined for you.

7. Cry for a change.

You can experience turn-around miracles only when you become desperate enough to cry for a change. Blind Bartimaeus needed a turn-around miracle. He was fed up with his status as a blind beggar. He was so desperate that even when people tried to shut him up he did not listen to any of them.

And they came to Jericho: and as he went out of Jericho with his disciples and a great number of people, blind Bartimaeus, the son of Timaeus, sat by the highway side begging. And when he heard that it was Jesus of Nazareth, he began to cry out, and say, Jesus, thou Son of David, have mercy on me. And many charged him that he should hold his peace: but he cried the more a great deal, Thou Son of David, have mercy on me. And Jesus stood still, and commanded him to be called. And they call the blind man, saying unto him, Be of good comfort, rise; he calleth thee. And he, casting away his garment, rose, and came to Jesus. And Jesus answered and said unto him, What wilt thou that I should do unto thee? The blind man said unto him, Lord, that I might receive my sight. And Jesus said unto him, Go thy way; thy faith hath made thee whole. And immediately he received his sight, and followed

CONNECTING TO THE GOD OF BREAKTHROUGHS (57)

Jesus in the way. (Mar 10:46-52)

The more they tried to stop Bartimaeus the more he increased his voice. He knew what he had gone through, sitting by the roadside begging. He was determined to make use of this opportunity. Incidentally his cry attracted the attention of Jesus Christ. Until you cry for a change your solution will remain the same. If you are satisfied with the status quo, you will never experience a change. You need to cry like a wounded lion. You must turn your voice to thunder, in order to get out of the valley.

Your voice is your weapon. Don't let the devil take it away from you. Shout until you experience a divine turn-around. Cry out, shout.

Let your voice scare the enemy. Let your cry attract the attention of Jesus. Cry, even if your voice would become hoarse; The moment you experience a breakthrough you will forget that you ever lost your voice. Pray until your change comes.

THE MOMENT OF CHANGE

You must make use of all these keys if you want the turn-around breakthrough that will give you the desires of your heart. Once the keys begin to work for you, keep using them. Keep using them until you move from one level of breakthrough to another. God is ready to turn your situation around.

This is your moment of change. This is the hour of your total transformation. God has promised to do a new thing in your life. Your story will change. Your star will shine. Your destiny must be fulfilled. God is ready to give you a pleasant surprise. The God of the suddenlies is waiting for you at your place of prayer. He will surprise you today.

Other Publications by Dr. D. K. Olukoya

1. A-Z of Complete Deliverance
2. Be Prepared
3. Bewitchment must die
4. Biblical Principles of Dream Interpretation
5. Born Great, But Tied Down
6. Breaking Bad Habits
7. Breakthrough Prayers For Business Professionals
8. Brokenness
9. Bringing Down The Power of God
10. Can God?
11. Can God Trust You?
12. Command The Morning
13. Consecration Commitment & Loyalty
14. Contending For The Kingdom
15. Connecting to The God of Breakthroughs
16. Criminals In The House Of God
17. Dealing With Hidden Curses
18. Dealing With Local Satanic Technology
19. Dealing With Satanic Exchange
20. Dealing With The Evil Powers Of Your Father's House
21. Dealing With Tropical Demons
22. Dealing With Unprofitable Roots
23. Dealing With Witchcraft Barbers
24. Deliverance By Fire
25. Deliverance From Spirit Husband And Spirit Wife
26. Deliverance From The Limiting Powers

Other Publications by Dr. D. K. Olukoya

27. Deliverance of The Brain
28. Deliverance Of The Conscience
29. Deliverance Of The Head
30. Deliverance: God's Medicine Bottle
31. Destiny Clinic
32. Disgracing Soul Hunters
33. Divine Military Training
34. Divine Yellow Card
35. Dominion Prosperity
36. Drawers Of Power From The Heavenlies
37. Evil Appetite
38. Evil Umbrella
39. Facing Both Ways
40. Failure In The School Of Prayer
41. Fire For Life's Journey
42. For We Wrestle ...
43. Freedom Indeed
44. Holiness Unto The Lord
45. Holy Cry
46. Holy Fever
47. Hour Of Decision
48. How To Obtain Personal Deliverance
49. How To Pray When Surrounded By The Enemies
50. Idols Of The Heart
51. Is This What They Died For?
52. Let God Answer By Fire
53. Limiting God

Other Publications by Dr. D. K. Olukoya

54. Madness Of The Heart
55. Making Your Way Through The Traffic Jam of Life
56. Meat For Champions
57. Medicine For Winners
58. My Burden For The Church
59. Open Heavens Through Holy Disturbance
60. Overpowering Witchcraft
61. Paralysing The Riders And The Horse
62. Personal Spiritual Check-Up
63. Power Against Coffin Spirits
64. Power Against Destiny Quenchers
65. Power Against Dream Criminals
66. Power Against Local Wickedness
67. Power Against Marine Spirits
68. Power Against Spiritual Terrorists
69. Power Must Change Hands
70. Pray Your Way To Breakthroughs
71. Prayer Is The Battle
72. Prayer Rain
73. Prayer Strategies For Spinsters And Bachelors
74. Prayer To Kill Enchantment
75. Prayer To Make You Fulfil Your Divine Destiny
76. Prayer Warfare Against 70 Mad Spirits
77. Prayers For Open Heavens
78. Prayers To Destroy Diseases And Infirmities
79. Prayers To Move From Minimum To Maximum
80. Praying Against The Spirit Of The Valley

Other Publications by Dr. D. K. Olukoya

81. Praying To Destroy Satanic Roadblocks
82. Praying To Dismantle Witchcraft
83. Principles Of Prayer
84. Release From Destructive Covenants
85. Revoking Evil Decrees
86. Safeguarding Your Home
87. Satanic Diversion Of The Black Race
88. Silencing The Birds Of Darkness
89. Slaves Who Love Their Chains
90. Smite The Enemy And He Will Flee
91. Speaking Destruction Unto The Dark Rivers
92. Spiritual Education
93. Spiritual Growth And Maturity
94. Spiritual Warfare And The Home
95. Strategic Praying
96. Strategy Of Warfare Praying
97. Students In The School Of Fear
98. Symptoms Of Witchcraft Attack
99. The Baptism of Fire
100. The Battle Against The Spirit Of Impossibility
101. The Dinning Table Of Darkness
102. The Enemy Has Done This
103. The Evil Cry Of Your Family Idol
104. The Fire Of Revival
105. The Great Deliverance
106. The Internal Stumbling Block
107. The Lord Is A Man Of War

Other Publications by Dr. D. K. Olukoya

108. The Mystery Of Mobile Curses
109. The Mystery Of The Mobile Temple
110. The Prayer Eagle
111. The Pursuit Of Success
112. The Seasons Of Life
113. The Secrets Of Greatness
114. The Serpentine Enemies
115. The Skeleton In Your Grandfather's Cupboard
116. The Slow Learners
117. The Snake In The Power House
118. The Spirit Of The Crab
119. The star hunters
120. The Star In Your Sky
121. The Tongue Trap
122. The Unconquerable Power
123. The Vagabond Spirit
124. The Way Of Divine Encounter
125. The Wealth Transfer Agenda
126. Tied Down In The Spirits
127. Too Hot To Handle
128. Turnaround Breakthrough
129. Unprofitable Foundations
130. Vacancy For Mad Prophets
131. Victory Over Satanic Dreams
132. Victory Over Your Greatest Enemies
133. Violent Prayers Against Stubborn Situations
134. War At The Edge Of Breakthroughs

Other Publications by Dr. D. K. Olukoya

135. Wasting The Wasters
136. Wealth Must Change Hands
137. What You Must Know About The House Fellowship
138. When God Is Silent
139. When the Battle is from Home
140. When The Deliverer Need Deliverance
141. When Things Get Hard
142. When You Are Knocked Down
143. Where Is Your Faith
144. While Men Slept
145. Woman! Thou Art Loosed.
146. Your Battle And Your Strategy
147. Your Foundation And Destiny
148. Your Mouth And Your Deliverance

YORUBA PUBLICATIONS
1. ADURA AGBAYORI
2. ADURA TI NSI OKE NIDI
3. OJO ADURA

FRENCH PUBLICATIONS
1. PLUIE DE PRIERE
2. ESPIRIT DE VAGABONDAGE
3. EN FINIR AVEC LES FORCES MALEFIQUES DE LA MAISON DE TON PERE
4. QUE I'ENVOUTEMENT PERISSE
5. FRAPPEZ I'ADVERSAIRE ET IL FUIRA

Other Publications by Dr. D. K. Olukoya

6. COMMENT RECEVIOR LA DELIVRANCE DU MARI ET FEMME DE NUIT
7. CPMMENT SE DELIVRER SOI-MEME
8. POVOIR CONTRE LES TERRORITES SPIRITUEL
9. PRIERE DE PERCEES POUR LES HOMMES D'AFFAIRES
10. PRIER JUSQU'A REMPORTER LA VICTOIRE
11. PRIERES VIOLENTES POUR HUMILIER LES PROBLEMES OPINIATRES
12. PRIERE POUR DETRUIRE LES MALADIES ET INFIRMITES
13. LE COMBAT SPIRITUEL ET LE FOYER
14. BILAN SPIRITUEL PERSONNEL
15. VICTOIRES SUR LES REVES SATANIQUES
16. PRIERES DE COMAT CONTRE 70 ESPIRITS DECHANINES
17. LA DEVIATION SATANIQUE DE LA RACE NOIRE
18. TON COMBAT ET TA STRATEGIE
19. VOTRE FONDEMENT ET VOTRE DESTIN
20. REVOQUER LES DECRETS MALEFIQUES
21. CANTIQUE DES CONTIQUES
22. LE MAUVAIS CRI DES IDOLES
23. QUAND LES CHOSES DEVIENNENT DIFFICILES
24. LES STRATEGIES DE PRIERES POUR LES CELIBATAIRES
25. SE LIBERER DES ALLIANCES MALEFIQUES
26. DEMANTELER LA SORCELLERIE
27. LA DELIVRANCE: LE FLACON DE MEDICAMENT DIEU
28. LA DELIVRANCE DE LA TETE
29. COMMANDER LE MATIN
30. NE GRAND MAIS LIE

Other Publications by Dr. D. K. Olukoya

31. POUVOIR CONTRE LES DEMOND TROPICAUX
32. LE PROGRAMME DE TRANFERT DE RICHESSE
33. LES ETUDIANTS A I'ECOLE DE LA PEUR
34. L'ETOILE DANS VOTRE CIEL
35. LES SAISONS DE LA VIE
36. FEMME TU ES LIBEREE

ANNUAL 70 DAYS PRAYER AND FASTING PUBLICATIONS

1. Prayers That Bring Miracles
2. Let God Answer By Fire
3. Prayers To Mount With Wings As Eagles
4. Prayers That Bring Explosive Increase
5. Prayers For Open Heavens
6. Prayers To Make You Fulfil Your Divine Destiny
7. Prayers That Make God To Answer And Fight By Fire
8. Prayers That Bring Unchallengeable Victory And Breakthrough Rainfall Bombardments
9. Prayers That Bring Dominion Prosperity And Uncommon Success
10. Prayers That Bring Power And Overflowing Progress
11. Prayers That Bring Laughter And Enlargement Breakthroughs
12. Prayers That Bring Uncommon Favour And Breakthroughs
13. Prayers That Bring Unprecedented Greatness & Unmatchable Increase
14. Prayers That Bring Awesome Testimonies And Turn Around Breakthroughs